You Are Here

you are here

Daniel MacIvor

You Are Here
first published 2002 by
Scirocco Drama
An imprint of J. Gordon Shillingford Publishing Inc.
© 2001 Daniel MacIvor

Scirocco Drama Editor: Glenda MacFarlane
Cover design by Terry Gallagher/Doowah Design Inc.
Author photo by Guntar Kravis
Printed and bound in Canada

We acknowledge the financial support of The Canada Council for the Arts
and the Manitoba Arts Council for our publishing program.

Production inquiries should be addressed to:
da da kamera
401 Richmond St. West, #356
Toronto, Ontario M5V 3A8
Phone: (416) 586-1503
Fax: (416) 586-1504

Canadian Cataloguing in Publication Data

MacIvor, Daniel, 1962-
        You are here/Daniel MacIvor
A play.
ISBN 1-896239-90-0
        I. Title.
PS8575.I86Y68 2002   C812'.54   C2002-902617-2
PR9199.3.M3225Y68 2002

J. Gordon Shillingford Publishing
P.O. Box 86, 905 Corydon Avenue, Winnipeg, MB Canada R3M 3S3

For Mira Friedlander

Acknowledgements

You Are Here was developed with the National Theatre School of Canada, Towson University, and the Millenium Arts Fund through The Canada Council for the Arts. Special thanks go to Maureen LaBonté, Perry Schneiderman and the students in the NTS graduating class of 2000: Amy Rutherford, Jonathan Eliot, Rowan Tichenor, Amy Stewart, Luke Kirby, Jocelyn Grover, Diana Donnelly, Rafal Sokolowski, Jamie Burnett, Kevin Vorey, Allan Hawco, and Alicia Johnston.

Daniel MacIvor

Daniel MacIvor has been creating drama since 1986. He is a writer/ performer/director and Artistic Director of da da kamera, a Toronto based international touring company he runs with Sherrie Johnson. His plays include *Somewhere I Have Never Travelled* at the Tarragon Theatre in Toronto; *Yes I Am and Who Are You?*, *See Bob Run*, and *2-2-Tango* at Buddies In Bad Times Theatre in Toronto; *Wild Abandon* and *Never Swim Alone* at Theatre Passe Muraille in Toronto; *This Is A Play* with the Fringe Festival of Toronto; *Marion Bridge* with Mulgrave Road Theatre in Guysborough, Nova Scotia; and *The Soldier Dreams* and *In On It* with da da kamera in Toronto. da da kamera has also produced the work he has created with long-time collaborator Daniel Brooks including *House*, *Here Lies Henry*, *The Lorca Play*, *Monster* and *Cul-de-sac*. da da kamera has produced his work in the United States, Israel, Australia, Norway, the UK and throughout Canada. His awards include an Over All Excellence at the 1999 New York Fringe Festival for *Never Swim Alone* and a 2001 GLAD award (from the American Gay and Lesbian Anti-Defamation League) and a 2001 *Village Voice* OBIE Award for da da kamera's production of *In On It* which opened at New York's PS 122 on September 27, 2001.

Notes

For me, *You Are Here* is a one woman show with twelve characters. The central relationship in the play is between Alison and the audience—a relationship which only begins to deteriorate when she meets Justin and loses her connection with herself and the audience. The only characters who speak to the audience are the characters who are dead: Richard, Connie Hoy and Alison, but it is always Alison's presence on the stage in front of the audience which is the engine which drives the play. For this reason, it is important that the actress playing Alison must own the text profoundly—she needs to feel a fluidity with the "um" 's, the broken sentences, the repetitions—also must have a freedom in the moment to address any disruptions that may occur. The actress must be confident in her owning of Alison so that she may speak to the audience outside the written text. To claim a true presence in the room and not to address a ringing cell phone, a walk-out, a persistent cougher, is to undermine the fundamental conceit of the experience of the evening.

For our set design Andy Moro created a black box with a receding perspective, four sets of wings which were approximately thirty feet apart at the front of the stage, each set closer until the farthest upstage set were approximately ten feet apart. This allowed characters to appear and disappear quickly, almost magically.

Regarding the stage directions: I have made every effort to track the minimal props so that the production does not become cluttered and confused with unnecessary business. The play is meant to be performed with the utmost minimalism. This is not to say one is limited to the props and actions indicated but one must treat each glass, flower, ice cube and bottle as a fully present object with a simple and clear entrance, use, and exit.

Daniel MacIvor
Toronto, June, 2002

Production History

You Are Here received its mainstage premiere on September 20, 2001, as a da da kamera production (in association with Theatre Passe Muraille) at Theatre Passe Muraille, Toronto, with the following cast:

ALISON.. Caroline Gillis
RICHARD .... Jim Allodi
CONNIE HOY/FIRST A.D. .... Marjorie Chan
TED STEEVES/DOCTOR/WAITER........................ Ryan McVittie
JERRY .... David Jansen
DIANE DRAKE .... Fiona Highet
THOMAS ROMAN .... Randy Hughson
PAUL/JUSTIN .... Allan Hawco

Directed by Daniel MacIvor
Produced by Sherrie Johnson
Sound and Music Designed and Composed by Richard Feren
Set and Lighting Design by Andy Moro
Production Management by Lynanne Sparrow
Assistant Stage Management: Lynanne Sparrow
Assistant to the Producer: Kimberly Purtell

Act One

A chair sits on the darkened stage. ALISON, unlit but visible, walks out onto the stage. In her hands she holds a clear bottle filled with sand. The house lights slowly fade. She looks out into the Audience. She approaches the Audience. From the darkness she speaks.

ALISON: Are you...?

A light rises slowly on the chair.

Am I...?

ALISON notices the light on the chair.

Is this for me?

ALISON approaches the chair.

Am I supposed to...?

ALISON sits. She looks out into the Audience looking for direction; encouragement; a familiar face. She begins speaking, haltingly at first.

This is my bottle of sand. I thought you might like to see it. It's my one sort of spiritual type possession. It comes from a desert near the Dead Sea. The cradle of civilization. I got it on a trip I took there. Long ago... Thousands of years ago. Of course not "thousands" literally of course. I guess one should be careful in a place like this, regarding hyperbole and metaphor. You know, what are the rules anyway. I think it's probably best if we just stick to the facts. So... Yes, long ago, pre-University, late in the last century, I took a bit of a *"journey"* to *"find myself"* back when people used to do that. Do people still do that? I'm sure they do. I've been a little out of touch. Yes, so. I didn't succeed at finding myself on my *"journey"* but I did find this. The sand. Not the bottle. I mean I did find the bottle but I mean the sand didn't come in the bottle or anything. I mean I put it in the bottle. It wasn't like they had a kiosk or something, selling bottles of Dead Sea sand. But the bottle I got from a shop. Not as an empty bottle. It was full when I got it. It was a local wine. But the bottle of wine wasn't long in my possession before it was an empty bottle. As has always been the case with… Which perhaps makes the bottle more significant than the sand. In the big picture. Yes. Anyway. The big picture is what makes this to me somehow…important, because: in here, in this bottle, mixed with this sand is the blood and tears of ancient wars, and the sweat from the building of civilizations, and the very impressions of the footprints of our ancient— perhaps ancestors, searching for the Promised Land. All here in this bottle of sand. I didn't mean for that to rhyme. That was unintentional. Anyway. And I suppose it was not insignificant to me that this same sand was sand I had been standing upon, which I had chosen, which I had been running through my fingers. Which somehow through some mixture of DNA, placed me in that big picture. Somehow made me part of the bigger world. The world has always seemed so small to me. And in those moments I would consider this, and my place in it, and… Maybe I'm over-thinking things. Maybe it is just the bottle. Anyway. It's just one of those silly things that means something to me. You know how sometimes they ask people *"If your house was on fire and you could only rescue one thing what would it be?"* Well this would be my one thing. It's not like I would choose it over a cat if I had a cat—in a fire I'd choose the cat of course—I wouldn't choose a bottle of sand over a cat in a fire—if I had a cat—but I never did, have a cat. Or a fire for that matter. Anyway. I wrote something.

ALISON puts down the bottle and takes a piece of folded paper from her pocket and opens it as she speaks.

I was trying to think of something pithy—but I've always been too long-winded and too much of a Libra to be pithy. So I thought *"go for profound"* — but it becomes apparent quite quickly that the very notion of *"going for"* profound isn't going to get you anywhere very profound. You just find yourself on this endless, rolling ocean of cliche. *"Ocean of cliche."* That's probably the wrong metaphor. Something more ordered. Factory of cliche. *"Churning, spinning, something, factory of cliche."* Something like that. So too much talk for pithy and no profundity forthcoming I thought I'd keep with the *"P"* theme and go with poetic.

ALISON reads a few lines to herself.

But you know how sometimes you write something quickly and you don't have a chance to look it over carefully and then when you look at it later it just seems so... written. I've written a lot. For newspapers and magazines. It's how I've made my living. I wouldn't call myself a writer, though. I've never had that passionate—that kind of passion for writing where I felt, you know *"through my veins instead of blood flows ink"* or anything like that. Just a job. Celebrity profiles, Who's Hot Who's Not, What Ever Happened To, that sort of thing. No hidden novels or burning ambition.

ALISON sighs.

Maybe passion is the way to go. Maybe passion's what's important. I've always saved my passion for...love. Which is, what is that? Which is, you know, I say love or *"I love you"* or you know and someone else says: *"When you say 'I love you' you build a cage."* And maybe they're right. Maybe. It's just language. But some people would say

"Language is all we've got to go on." Of course they might contradict themselves later and say *"Language is just a vibration in the diaphragm which happens as a result of our response to the idea of the self as an entity separate from the thing we call me."* I'm getting too specific. That was always one of my weaknesses as a journalist. That and simply telling the story.

ALISON laughs weakly. She considers the piece of paper she still holds in her hand. She puts it away.

My friend Richard used to say: *"The story knows more than you do, let the story tell itself."* Which sounds good but... And anyway I'm not even sure where he got that advice, or more importantly why I should trust it. Knowing Richard. Richard and I met sharing a house in University. I was studying journalism, he was studying to be a social anthropologist but his chosen course of study was more *"social"* than *"pologist"*.

RICHARD speaks from off stage.

RICHARD: *(Off stage.)* Alison! Listen to this.

ALISON: Richard?

RICHARD appears carrying a notebook and wearing a wildly colourful vest which was the height of style about thirty years ago. He faces out and away from ALISON as he speaks to her. RICHARD reads from the book he carries.

RICHARD: *"The mortal's taste is so fickle, their character so hypocritical, their judgements so wrongheaded, that those persons who pleasantly and blithely indulge their inclinations seem to be very much better off than those who torment themselves with anxiety."* Sir Thomas More.

ALISON: *(To Audience.)* Richard thought I tormented myself with anxiety.

RICHARD: It's pretty good huh?

ALISON: What's it for?

RICHARD: It's for my book.

ALISON: What book?

RICHARD: My book! My book of quotes.

ALISON: What?

RICHARD: *"Live Fast Die Old"*. My book of quotes I've been working on.

ALISON: Oh that.

RICHARD: Duh. Yeah that. Steeves said he'd help me with it. He said North Americans need any reminders they can get to stop worrying and enjoy life. Steeves gave me this quote.

ALISON: Steeves. *(To the Audience.)* Ted Steeves. Taught Art History. Wore leather. Screwed his students. Pushed a philosophy of indulgence.

RICHARD: It's not about indulgence. It's about the fact that most people are such high-strung, up-tight, over-achieving assholes that the poor mindless shits who just live and don't get all worked up about it are better off.

ALISON: And who are the poor mindless shits?

RICHARD: The poor mindless shits.

ALISON: Not us?

RICHARD: We should aspire to poor mindless shitdom.

ALISON: *(To Audience.)* That was so exactly Steeves. *(To RICHARD.)* That is so exactly Steeves.

RICHARD: I thought you liked Steeves.

ALISON: He's a pig.

RICHARD: Since when?

ALISON: Since he's screwing Connie Hoy.

RICHARD: Steeves is screwing Connie Hoy?

ALISON: Yes.

RICHARD: Cool.

ALISON: Connie Hoy is a student.

RICHARD: She's his teaching assistant.

ALISON: She's a student of the University.

RICHARD: She's not his student.

ALISON: Connie Hoy grosses me out.

RICHARD: Connie Hoy can gross me out any time.

ALISON: You are such a man.

RICHARD: Is that supposed to be an insult?

ALISON: Yes.

RICHARD: Come on let's go to the party.

ALISON: I'm not going to any party.

RICHARD: Alison!

ALISON: A bunch of hockey players and cheerleaders.

RICHARD: This afternoon you were like *"Oh it's going to be a great party, I'm going to wear something sexy."*

ALISON: Yeah well it's not this afternoon anymore.

RICHARD: Maybe you'll meet somebody.

ALISON: I don't want to meet somebody.

RICHARD: Come on there'll be lots of nice guys there.

ALISON: What's a *"nice guy"*? What's *"nice"*?

RICHARD: I don't know, quiet, smart, you know, fun kind of but not too wild. I don't know, nice.

ALISON: So would you consider yourself a nice guy?

RICHARD: I'm more of, more of, like a dandy.

ALISON: A what?

RICHARD: Or like a cad sort of but in an adorable way.

ALISON: *"Nice".* It seems to me that "nice" is a word used to describe adequate. I'm not interested in adequate.

RICHARD: I don't know. Nice might be amazing. That's what I'm looking for—just a little something nice.

ALISON: Nice is boring.

RICHARD: Look this is boring. Put on something sexy and let's go. I'll lust after some cheerleaders and you can fall in love some nice guy. Or not. Flirt with some hockey players. Let's just go. Fuck it's Friday night!

ALISON: The time when all good mindless shits go out and indulge their inclinations.

RICHARD: Yeah.

ALISON: No thanks.

RICHARD: At least we can get drunk.

ALISON: I can get drunk on my own thank you very much.

RICHARD: No fun.

RICHARD disappears. ALISON speaks to the Audience.

ALISON: *"Temptations can be got rid of...by giving into them."* Balzac.

She looks off where RICHARD departed.

ALISON: I forgot that book. But other things I remember. That ridiculous vest. Connie Hoy. I always had a thing about Connie Hoy. She was one of those girls... But we don't need to get into that. And we certainly don't need to get into Ted Steeves.

> *TED STEEVES appears. A young dapper professor. He speaks out and away from ALISON as RICHARD did.*

TED: Alison?

ALISON: Oh no.

TED: How are you doing?

ALISON: Fine.

TED: Thanks again for dinner.

ALISON: Oh right well no yes thanks.

TED: The pie was delicious.

ALISON: Oh you know.

TED: Anyway. I just wanted to say—

ALISON: Oh that's fine don't worry about it.

TED: Don't worry about what?

ALISON: Whatever it was you were going to say, it's fine.

TED: Oh...'kay. How was Richard's trip?

ALISON: Good. Good.

TED: What do people do in Niagara Falls in the winter?

ALISON: Search me.

TED: You haven't been in class this week.

ALISON: I've been you know...

TED: Are you okay?

ALISON:	Of course.
	CONNIE HOY enters.
CONNIE:	Ted? Oh hi Alison.
ALISON:	Hi Connie.
CONNIE:	*(To TED.)* I was waiting. Should I…?
TED:	No sure I'm just coming now.
ALISON:	Bye.
CONNIE:	I like your hair, you did something to it.
ALISON:	No, it's the same.
CONNIE:	*(To ALISON.)* How's Richard?
ALISON:	Fine fine.
CONNIE:	Sharon's been asking about him.
ALISON:	He's been you know busy.
CONNIE:	I heard he went to Niagara Falls.
ALISON:	Yeah.
CONNIE:	Crazy guy. Say hi for me.
TED:	Me too. And *he* hasn't been in class lately either.
	TED STEEVES leads CONNIE HOY out. ALISON speaks to the Audience.
ALISON:	I don't want to get into Ted Steeves.
	RICHARD appears carrying a drink.
RICHARD:	Steeves!
ALISON:	Richard…
RICHARD:	Steeves!?
ALISON:	Stop it.

RICHARD: Steeves!?

ALISON: Stop it. And what about Connie Hoy anyway. She's
             just gross.

RICHARD   Why's she gross?

ALISON: She's like one of those girls who goes to nursing
             school to marry a doctor.

RICHARD   A what?

ALISON: Her whole life is about the crock of the happy little
             home she's going to make with her happy little
             husband and her happy little brats. It's
             embarrassing.

RICHARD   Connie Hoy's going to nursing school?

ALISON: No! God! It's a type thing!

RICHARD   What's wrong with nurses?

ALISON: Richard!

                 A beat.

RICHARD   Steeves?!

ALISON: Stop it.

RICHARD   He's so tweedy!

ALISON: He is not.

RICHARD   You had him over for dinner?!

ALISON: Yes.

RICHARD   Steeves!

ALISON: Stop it.

RICHARD   And you told him I was in Niagara Falls?

ALISON: Yes.

RICHARD   Why?

ALISON: It was the first thing that came into my head.

RICHARD   Because that's where you and Steeves are going on your honeymoon!!!??

ALISON: Richard grow up.

RICHARD   Steeves!

ALISON: Stop it.

RICHARD   You made him dinner?!

ALISON: Yes.

            A Pause.

ALISON: And a pie.

RICHARD   No!

ALISON: From scratch.

RICHARD   Steeves!

            RICHARD disappears.

ALISON: Let me just say this about Steeves. Ted Steeves was the kind of professor who would read conspiracy theory to you, and show you slides of art you'd never seen before, and take you out to these amazing performances in dirty basements, and introduce you to books you felt at the time were changing your life, and occasionally take you out to fine wine bars and order in the language of the vineyard, and once he would come over to your place for dinner, and you would make a difficult chicken dish your roommate taught you and a pie from scratch, and over dinner you would get very very drunk and in the middle of dessert profess your love for him and he wouldn't know what to say but he would hold your head as you threw up into the toilet and then kiss you on the forehead in a kind of apology as he left. And let's call that the end of Ted Steeves. Which I would assume, considering the way things are going, would indicate the beginning of Jerry.

RICHARD: *(Off stage.)* Jerry!

RICHARD and JERRY enter holding drinks.

JERRY: How's your Dad?

RICHARD: Oh you know.

JERRY: Thank him again for Thanksgiving.

RICHARD: I haven't talked to him since then—he got so on my back, as usual.

JERRY: He just wanted to know if you actually got your degree or not.

RICHARD: Yeah yeah.

JERRY: And I don't even know. Did you?

RICHARD: Yeah no Jerry whatever no yeah no.

JERRY: Okay. It's just you were such an overachiever in high school and now—

RICHARD: I've got a lot on the go.

JERRY: You don't even wear a watch.

RICHARD: I don't like anything on my arms.

JERRY: Yeah but—

RICHARD: Can we move on to another topic? Please?

JERRY: Sure. Um. Have you been to the cottage since—

RICHARD: No no no, a specific topic.

JERRY: What?

RICHARD: You go.

JERRY: Well what?

RICHARD: Specifically something about someone maybe?

JERRY: Someone?

RICHARD: Specifically someone you maybe met recently, at specifically Thanksgiving maybe, at my specifically Dad's?

JERRY: Oh Alison!

RICHARD: Bingo. Why don't you ask me some questions about Alison.

JERRY: Okay. Is she seeing anyone?

RICHARD: Excellent question. No she's not.

JERRY: All right. Is she interested in me?

RICHARD: Excellent question. Yes she is.

JERRY: Oh so she knew you were seeing me today and asked that you mention her.

RICHARD: Yes but that's not a question. Keep going.

JERRY: Okay. Um—

RICHARD: What is she doing tonight?

JERRY: Am I asking you that?

RICHARD: Yes you are. Tonight? Well as a matter of fact I'm meeting her later—she just got a job and we're celebrating. Perhaps you'd like to join the celebration?

JERRY: Perhaps. And what does the mysterious Alison do?

RICHARD: Oh the mysterious Alison! The messenger thanks you for such an excellent phrase to return with.

JERRY: Well she was mysterious. She barely said anything about herself.

RICHARD: That's *'best behaviour'*. Don't get used to that.

JERRY: So you're not interested in her? I thought maybe you and she were…

RICHARD: No! No I know her too well.

JERRY: Is that a negative thing?

RICHARD: It's a friends thing.

JERRY: Have you slept with her?

RICHARD: What?

JERRY: No I mean just have you?

RICHARD: What difference does it make?

JERRY: I'm asking questions.

RICHARD: Well I don't want to answer that question.

JERRY: So you did?

RICHARD: I don't want to ruin your sacrifice to the volcano or whatever you're planning but I don't think she's a virgin Jerry if that's what—

JERRY: I'm asking if you slept with her.

             ALISON moves away, looking off, no longer listening.

RICHARD: Why does it matter?

JERRY: You're my friend.

RICHARD: I think it's pretty weird that it should matter.

JERRY: I just want to know.

RICHARD: Would it make some incredible difference if I did? Would it stop you from pursuing something?

JERRY: It might.

RICHARD: No. I didn't.

JERRY: You did!

RICHARD: No! Jesus! I think Mister Psychiatrist should do a little on himself.

JERRY: I'm a psychologist not a psychiatrist.

RICHARD: Whatever you are take a pill.

> *RICHARD and JERRY disappear. ALISON speaks to the Audience.*

ALISON: Yes. So. Anyway. Let's not talk about Jerry. Let's talk about *Charles*.

> *DIANE DRAKE appears. A sexy young starlet. She sits, waiting impatiently.*

That's not *Charles*. *Charles* was the name of a magazine. On the cover under *Charles* it described itself as "*A Very Magazine*". And it was, very "*Very*". *Charles* was where I spent the bulk of my brilliant career. At *Charles* I had the opportunity to interview many fascinating and famous people. Fascinating people were always fascinating and famous people were always…well, famous. *(ALISON looks out, speaking to DIANE, DIANE looks out as she speaks to ALISON.)* Diane.

DIANE: Pardon me?

ALISON: Miss Drake.

DIANE: Okay so, first of all I do not want to talk about the clinic. I'm here to talk about the film.

ALISON: Fine.

DIANE: *Nadia's Body.*

ALISON: Okay.

DIANE: And I don't want to talk about the clinic. It's the

| | story everybody wants but they're not getting it because there is no story. |

ALISON: Okay.

DIANE: And that's all I want to say.

ALISON: That's all you want to say?

DIANE: About the clinic. Because there's no story.

ALISON: Okay. So. *Nadia's Body* was shot in Toronto. Did you enjoy working in Canada?

DIANE: Oh Canada is so great.

ALISON: And why is that?

DIANE: Because it just is. Like people say that Canadians are boring or like prudish or something but they're so not. Everyone is major fun and cute.

ALISON: Are you familiar with the concept of the Canadian mosaic versus the American melting pot?

DIANE: Uh huh.

ALISON: Do you think there's anything to it?

DIANE: Uh huh. Like the way I see things is that I am a very spiritual person. And that ultimately we're all connected.

ALISON: Uh huh...so how do you bring that philosophy to your films?

DIANE: Which films?

ALISON: Any of your films.

DIANE: All my films are so different but I learn so much from each one of them.

           A beat.

ALISON: But *Nadia's Body* is a radical departure from the work you were doing with Thomas Roman.

A beat.

DIANE: All my films are so different but I learn so much from each one of them.

ALISON: I was wondering how you felt about the nudity.

DIANE: Oh the nudity the nudity, why does everyone want to talk about the nudity? I'm so sick of talking about the nudity.

ALISON: Well you are nude for the entire film.

DIANE: It's called *Nadia's Body*—I'm Nadia and here's her body. Big deal.

ALISON: Okay.

DIANE: It's just like all right…I'm a very sexual person, it's part of me as an actress and of my personality and I think that it's important to use all my parts… *(She laughs.)* of me…of my personality. Right.

ALISON: Will you continue to do work like the edgy work you were doing with Thomas Roman?

DIANE: What do you mean by edgy?

ALISON: Um. Raw.

DIANE: Raw. Cheap you mean.

ALISON: It's about esthetic.

DIANE: It's about budget.

ALISON: Not only.

DIANE: Only.

ALISON: But a film like Roman's *The Wife of Hector Finch* doesn't compare to a film like *Nadia's Body*.

DIANE: In what way does it not compare.

ALISON: In any way.

DIANE: Well, taste is in the mouth of the you know…taster.

ALISON: It's not about taste.

DIANE: Nobody liked *Hector Finch*.

ALISON: It was a wonderful film.

DIANE: Didn't you find it confusing? There were three wives all totally different but all supposed to be the same person. And sometimes we were all in the same scene.

ALISON: It didn't follow a linear narrative line no.

DIANE: It didn't make any sense.

ALISON: Well surely you discussed it with Roman, you were living with him at the time.

DIANE: What magazine do you work for?

ALISON: *Charles*.

DIANE: Is that a tabloid?

ALISON: No it's—

DIANE: Good. Look. Thomas is a lovely guy, but he's got this weird process where you just throw the idea up in the air and everybody runs with it. I don't like that, I like to be told what to do. I don't want to have the idea I just want to borrow it. But that's Thomas, he's an artist. I'm not an artist, I'm an actress.

ALISON: But you have to agree that the scene with the couple on the bridge—

DIANE: I don't have to agree with anything. Look, some people like things they don't understand and some people like to understand things. It's a free world. Anyway. That's probably it, I better get going.

ALISON: When I was doing my research I found something online you might be interested in.

DIANE: What?

ALISON: A movie. I watched it. I found it through a link from a Japanese fan site.

DIANE: Which movie?

ALISON: Apparently it's very hard to find.

DIANE: Oh yeah?

ALISON: *Santa's Postman.*

DIANE: What? *Santa's Postman.* Oh my God.

ALISON: I'll send the information to your publicist.

DIANE: Oh my God! They're unfindable. It was the first film I ever did. It was when my Mom was my manager— it was the first job she got me. Oh my God.

ALISON: You were very cute.

DIANE: I was eight. I was so excited—we shot for two months in Greenland. Cold? Gosh! But it was so exciting. I had two lines. *"It's a very important letter for Santa."* and...

ALISON: *"It looks like there's going to be a Christmas after all."*

DIANE: Yes!

ALISON: And you were right.

DIANE: Huh?

ALISON: There was a Christmas after all.

DIANE: Yeah there was... And that's the thing see, like I loved my Mom so much and she was such a great manager and when she died I was just so...you know...and I fell in with a bad agency and into the modelling thing and you might as well disfigure your face with a broken bottle as gain a pound right?

ALISON: Uh huh.

DIANE: Which is I guess how it all started I guess, when I look at it now. That whole thing with the clinic and all that. See it wasn't a drug thing, it was an eating disorder thing.

ALISON: But you got through it though, you survived.

DIANE: Yeah, I did.

ALISON: It takes a lot of courage to survive, a lot of young women would really look up to you if they knew.

DIANE: Do you want to keep talking?

ALISON: Sure.

            DIANE rises to leave.

DIANE: I'll just tell my driver. *(Turning back.)* Thanks.

            DIANE exits.

ALISON: *(Calling after her.)* No thank you. Thank you for playing the game, thank you for pretending to believe my generosity exceeded beyond the thousand dollars I spent tracking down that stupid movie, thank you for showing me just how well the game could work.

            (To the Audience.) That was my first cover story. It was supposed to be a page sixty-four "What's Up With So and So" type thing. But I got the story everybody wanted and I got bigger desk, and better assignments, and entry into a world where other people's misfortune was a cause for celebration, where relationships were built on disdain, where air kisses replaced hugs and talent wasn't in the least important as long as you had good tits and a really fabulous pair of shoes. Thanks for that. And most of all thank you for the anger. Because as we all know, anger is a gift.

JERRY appears. ALISON does not look at him.
JERRY speaks to ALISON. ALISON does not look at
him.

JERRY: Anger is a gift.

ALISON: I know.

JERRY: Use your anger. If there's one thing that seems to
            hold people back it's an inability to use their anger
            constructively. Your capacity for anger is equal to
            your ability for action.

ALISON: I know.

JERRY: Look at me.

            JERRY approaches ALISON.

ALISON: Why?

JERRY: Just look at me.

ALISON: Why?

JERRY: So I can look at you.

            JERRY takes ALISON in his arms and turns her to
            him. ALISON looks at him.

            You're so fantastic.

ALISON: I read your story.

JERRY: You're so fantastic.

ALISON: I liked it. You're a good writer.

JERRY: I'm not a writer I'm a psychologist.

ALISON: You could be a writer if you wanted to be.

JERRY: I wrote that story for you.

ALISON: You wrote it before you met me.

JERRY: And still I wrote it for you.

           You Are Here

ALISON: You're such a goof.

JERRY: A goof for you.

                 ALISON moves to leave his embrace.

ALISON: I should go.

                 JERRY holds her more tightly.

JERRY: No.

ALISON: *(Laughing.)* Jerry. I have to get up in the morning. Let me go. What time is it?

JERRY: Guess and I'll let you go.

ALISON: Three…fifteen.

JERRY: Sorry, three twelve.

ALISON: I was close.

JERRY: Close only counts in horseshoes and hand grenades.

ALISON: And elevators.

                 JERRY laughs.

JERRY: And elevators. Mmmm.

ALISON: I have to go.

JERRY: Kiss me two more times.

                 ALISON does. JERRY doesn't let her go.

ALISON: Jerry.

JERRY: Kiss me three more times.

                 ALISON does. JERRY doesn't let her go.

ALISON: Jerry?

JERRY: Kiss me twelve more times.

ALISON: I have to go.

JERRY: Stay.

ALISON: I'm practically living here.

JERRY: Live here. Move in.

ALISON: Jerry no.

JERRY: You're fantastic.

ALISON: Stop it.

JERRY: You're fantastic.

ALISON: I have to go.

JERRY: No stay and we'll lock the door and unplug the phone and cover the windows with tinfoil so that the sun will never come up and time will pass us by. Time won't ever know we're here.

ALISON: Jerry.

JERRY: Sh! We have to be very very quiet so time won't find us. That way we can just be like this forever. Just like this. Nothing can change from this. From you looking like that and me feeling like this.

                A beat. JERRY lets her go and stands behind her.

ALISON: What?

JERRY: Marry me.

                JERRY disappears. ALISON speaks to the Audience.

ALISON: It's interesting how he said *"Marry me."* He didn't say *"Will you marry me?"* or *"Let's get married."* or *"You know I was thinking about it and I thought we might get married. What do you think?"* No. He said *"Marry me."* Like it was a directive. As if I didn't have a choice; *"Marry me,"* not something we'd do together but something I was supposed to do to him: like *"love me"* or *"feed me"* or *"burp me."* And I never wanted to get married. Ever. Even as a girl. I was never deluded about the romance of a sit-down dinner for seventy-five or a twelve-hundred dollar prom dress. Or veils. We got past the horse-drawn carriage and the trousseau but we never got past the veil. I was never the marrying type. That was Connie Hoy. Marriage always made me think of Connie Hoy. Who by the way eventually ended up marrying Ted Steeves and having a vanload of kids. But that was Connie Hoy, and I was not Connie Hoy. I was an independent woman and I was going to have an interesting life. Leave marriage to the Connie Hoys of the world, I never wanted to get married.

> *RICHARD appears carrying a flower, a drink with an ice cube and a shawl.*

RICHARD   Then don't get married.

ALISON: When did you say that?

RICHARD   You let the fire go out.

ALISON: Sorry?

RICHARD   I got it going again. Do you like it here?

ALISON: Here where?

RICHARD: Here on earth.

ALISON: What?

RICHARD: *(Laughing.)* At the cottage.

> *RICHARD throws the shawl to ALISON, she catches it and puts it on her shoulders. She sits on the floor.*

ALISON: Oh yes, the cottage, I love the cottage.

RICHARD: My Dad says he'll give it to me if I get married.

ALISON: That's incentive.

RICHARD: But I don't want the cottage. I'm not going to tell him that though or he might offer me something I want.

RICHARD takes a drink.

ALISON: What do you want?

RICHARD: I want to figure out how to make an ice cube that doesn't melt.

ALISON: Then it wouldn't be an ice cube.

RICHARD: What do you mean? If it's not melting it's not an ice cube?

ALISON: Melting is part of the process of the ice cube.

RICHARD: That's dark.

ALISON: What's dark about it?

RICHARD: You're not enjoying the ice cube.

ALISON: Ice cubes melt, that's their purpose.

RICHARD: No, ice cubes keep things cold, that's their purpose.

ALISON: But they do inevitably melt.

RICHARD holds up his glass.

RICHARD: Okay, so this sad little melting ice cube—this is an ice cube?

ALISON: Yes.

RICHARD: But the ice cube in the freezer that's not melting—isn't it still an ice cube?

ALISON: Freezing's just the other side of melting, it's the same thing.

RICHARD: It is not, how can you say that!

ALISON: Anyway it's all just water, ice is what we call the state of frozen water.

RICHARD:	You've just negated the existence of the ice cube! That is so dark.
ALISON:	Sorry that's life.
RICHARD:	With an attitude like that you definitely shouldn't get married.
ALISON:	Oh God, why didn't I listen to you.
RICHARD:	When I was in Japan I asked Shanti to marry me.
ALISON:	The teacher?
RICHARD:	No that was Shari, she was English. Shanti was Cambodian. The girl who was helping me with my photography.
ALISON:	The prostitute?
RICHARD:	Hostess.
ALISON:	What did she say?
RICHARD:	She said she'd marry me but we'd have to split up when her true love asked for her hand.
ALISON:	Where was her true love?
RICHARD:	She didn't know, she hadn't met him yet, she just knew he wasn't me.
ALISON:	Oh God.
RICHARD:	Do you love him?
ALISON:	Yes. No. I mean whatever that is. I don't know. Yes. No. I don't know.
RICHARD:	I hope you're more decisive about the guest list.
ALISON:	Guest lists, invitations, seventy-five people for dinner. I am not wearing a veil.
RICHARD:	Do you want to get married?
ALISON:	I don't.

RICHARD: Then don't.

ALISON: I mean I do but I don't.

RICHARD   Which is it?

ALISON: It's more the wedding that's bothering me than the marriage.

RICHARD   Then don't have a wedding.

ALISON: What are you saying? Cancel the wedding?

RICHARD   Why not?

ALISON: The invitations have been sent.

RICHARD   The invitations have been sent? Is that reason enough to have a wedding you don't want?

ALISON: Stop it.

             ALISON rises, taking off the shawl.

RICHARD: What I say is you should just screw the whole thing and run off with me to Mexico and get married. That's what you should do.

             ALISON looks at him. She has heard this line as if for the first time. She does not remember him saying this before. RICHARD looks at ALISON waiting for her to say her next line. A long moment passes. ALISON looks away.

RICHARD: You're supposed to laugh now.

             ALISON shoots him a look.

             This is the part where you laugh.

             ALISON walks past him, dropping the shawl in his lap, then stops facing upstage.

ALISON: Ha.

RICHARD: You'll have to do better than that.

ALISON: HA!

RICHARD: Get married, think of it as a party, have fun.

               *RICHARD rises, drops the flower on the chair and
               leaves. ALISON turns, looking after him.*

ALISON: Richard...

               *Now alone, ALISON sees the flower lying on the
               chair. She picks it up and studies it. She sits.*

               There's a scene near the end of the film *The Wife of
               Hector Finch* by the director Thomas Roman where
               Diane Drake as the young wife and the French actor
               Rene Voltair as Hector Finch run through a park
               laughing and in love. The wife runs on to a bridge
               over a river and Hector Finch catches her in his
               arms. He turns her around and gives her a flower.
               She smells the flower, she admires it, she smiles, she
               looks at Hector Finch and then gently rips the
               flower in half. She holds one half in her hand and
               gives him the other half. He takes the petals and
               gently, gently places them in his breast pocket
               pressing them lovingly into his heart. She takes her
               half of the flower and throws it into the river
               laughing. Hector Finch doesn't know whether or
               not to be hurt but forgets everything as his wife
               throws herself into his arms and we watch the petals
               float down the river.

               THOMAS ROMAN appears.

THOMAS: Yes. And?

ALISON: What... What um... What did you hope to say with
               that scene?

THOMAS: You're the critic you tell me.

ALISON: I'm not a critic I just ask people questions.

THOMAS: Perhaps we should talk about *Immediate Action*?

ALISON: Sorry?

THOMAS: The film we're here to talk about?

ALISON: Sorry. Yes. So. How does it feel to be working with Diane Drake again?

THOMAS: Wonderful.

ALISON: And?

THOMAS: What? You want better than wonderful? Or worse?

ALISON: Were you hoping to recreate the magic of the *Hector Finch* days by working with her again or—

THOMAS: I don't do magic I do movies. Are we here for *Hector Finch* or this film?

ALISON: Yes... Um ...

THOMAS: *Immediate Action.*

ALISON: Yes I know um... And in *Immediate Action* Diane Drake plays...

THOMAS: Celeste.

ALISON: Celeste. Yes. And the character of Celeste is in almost every scene.

THOMAS: Leads usually are yes.

ALISON: No of course yes. But I was curious if... Does your on-again off-again relationship with Diane Drake in any way hinder...or assist your—

THOMAS: Which relationship?

ALISON: Your romance.

THOMAS: Am I having a romance with Diane Drake?

ALISON: According to the press package—

THOMAS: And according to my mother I'm a bum. Let's talk about movies.

ALISON: Okay. Your last film before leaving America and

most of your European work remains largely unseen—and now you've taken a very deliberate step into the mainstream with this more accessible recent work.

THOMAS: This is a question?

ALISON: Sorry. A film like *Immediate Action* seems to be aiming for a different kind of audience—

THOMAS: Aiming? I'm not aiming at anything. Let's move on.

ALISON: It's clear you are a very gifted filmmaker and yet the American producers you've been—

THOMAS: Do you believe in God?

ALISON: In…

THOMAS: Do you?

ALISON: Not in a conventional sense.

THOMAS: So no?

ALISON: So… No.

THOMAS: And when you say I'm gifted, from whence does this gift come?

ALISON: Chance? I don't know.

THOMAS: In my work I'm embracing my own confusion, my own insignificance. There's no gift there is only insignificance.

ALISON: But your earlier films—

THOMAS: You critics! You critics! What is it you critics want!?

ALISON: I'm not a critic I just—

THOMAS: My early films! My early films! Let it go, they're gone, they were naive, they were simplistic, they were sentimental. No one wants to see these films! I have a house in California for my mother, I have a house in France for an ex-wife and two children, I have a shack in Italy for myself! I pay tax in three countries! I have to make money! I can't make these stupid films you people want to see! For God's sake you people!

A beat. ALISON begins to weep.

ALISON: I'm sorry.

THOMAS: Oh my God this is insane.

ALISON: I'm sorry.

THOMAS: Stop that now. Stop.

ALISON: Yes I'm sorry. Do you have a—

THOMAS produces a handkerchief.

Thank you.

THOMAS: I'm sorry I upset you.

ALISON: No, I'm sorry. I don't know what's wrong with me.

THOMAS: I just can't keep reading these stories of how I was so promising and now I'm so crap. Another story of my artistic decline.

ALISON: No that's not what—I'm a fan. Really. *Hector Finch* was such a beautiful film. And that scene on the bridge—it really spoke to me—it really made me feel something. Maybe that's what's wrong. I don't know. I got married recently and…

THOMAS: I see.

ALISON: No but everything's fine. It's fine. But when I think about that scene—how you really nailed the paradox—how we think we're supposed to keep the flower but really it's better if we throw the flower away. And not just the paradox of relationships but the paradox of life.

THOMAS:	If you like.
ALISON:	I'm sorry, I'm being ridiculous.
THOMAS:	It's a frightening thing. To throw the flower away. It goes against all our instincts. We want to keep the flower, to own it. We want to own it all, the flower, the sunset, the lover, the air we breathe. And with everything we own we become bigger and bigger. But so big, then we realize, inside all that big is so much space to feel empty. Better to face the truth and know we own nothing, we can only own nothing, and better that we should. *(A moment.)* This is nice. Nice to have some feeling in the room for a change. But of course this is just me getting old and you having a bad day.
ALISON:	The strange thing is I'm not really having a bad day.
THOMAS:	This is a good day?

ALISON laughs.

You know, for what it's worth? If I could see one good script? For nothing! I would do it for nothing. I see these scripts and oh my God! But this is what these producers pay me for, the idiots. Anyone can produce, you just have to be organized and know how to use a telephone. No but, the other way. Telephone first. Organized is negotiable.

ALISON laughs.

So we call the interview over?

ALISON:	Yes fine.
THOMAS:	Good. So now can I take you out? To dinner.
ALISON:	Take me out?
THOMAS:	Sure.
ALISON:	I don't think so.

THOMAS: You're very beautiful.

ALISON: I'm very married.

THOMAS: I'm very hungry.

ALISON laughs.

Shall I make the reservation?

A beat. ALISON revels in a moment of nostalgia.

What is it?

ALISON: Nothing. Yes, that would be nice.

THOMAS leaves. ALISON laughs at herself. ALISON's DOCTOR appears carrying a folder.

DOCTOR: Alison?

ALISON: Yes?

DOCTOR: I guess you came in for your test results.

ALISON: Sure.

DOCTOR: Not too much to report really— Oh yes, just a little thing. I do get a sense of why you've been so emotional lately.

ALISON: Yes. Right. Yes.

DOCTOR: You're pregnant.

ALISON: Yes I am.

DOCTOR: Yes you are.

ALISON: Yes I am.

DOCTOR: Congratulations.

ALISON: *(To the Audience.)* And yes and congratulations and yes. And it was like a door opened on a room I didn't even know I had. A room with an amazing view. For a little while I understood everything—

things made sense. Just my body even—just *The Human Body* suddenly, finally made sense to me. Things worked.

> *ALISON sees something across and just off-stage. She rises and moves toward it.*

(*To the Audience.*) What's this? What's this for. Is this for me?

> *ALISON reaches just off stage and picks up a glass tumbler containing a deep red liquid.*

What day is this? Wait. No. Is this that Monday? Is this that Monday morning? Don't I get a choice?

> *JERRY enters and sits reading a newspaper.*

JERRY: Good morning.

ALISON: Good morning.

JERRY: What's that?

ALISON: I made you some beet juice.

JERRY: I'm on a fast.

ALISON: You can drink juice on a fast.

JERRY: No thanks.

ALISON: I didn't sleep at all last night.

JERRY: Was he moving around a lot?

ALISON: No "*she*" wasn't.

JERRY: I just don't want to say "*it*".

ALISON: Why always "*he*"? Why never "*she*"?

JERRY: I don't know why we just didn't go ahead and let them tell us at the ultrasound and avoid all this.

ALISON: Avoid all this what?

JERRY:	This banal banter.
ALISON:	Sorry. I'll try and be more stimulating.
JERRY:	Good morning darling.
ALISON:	Good morning darling.
JERRY:	I'm sorry you didn't sleep well.
ALISON:	If somebody told me I was going to end up in a relationship where we called one another darling I would never have believed it.
JERRY:	Well what would you like me to call you? Dear? Honey? Baby? Sweetie? Fuckbucket?
ALISON:	Fuckbucket. Yeah call me fuckbucket.
JERRY:	That's funny: *"end up"*. That's funny.
ALISON:	End up what?
JERRY:	You said you never thought you'd *"end up"* in a relationship where you said darling. What is this *"end up"*? Have we *"ended up"*? Is this the end of something? What's ended?
ALISON:	It's just a figure of speech, don't analyze everything to death.
JERRY:	It's language. It's all we've got to go on. Fuckbucket.
ALISON:	No, there's also action. And as the saying goes action speaks louder.
JERRY:	The importance of action does not negate the importance of language... God I hate when you do that.
ALISON:	Do what?
JERRY:	These broad... These eliminative comparisons.
ALISON:	Sorry? *"Eliminative"*? I pity your poor patients.

JERRY: Ha!

ALISON: What?

JERRY: Pity away. My patience. My poor patience. My challenged virtue.

ALISON: Once upon a time I would have found that cute, now I just want to hit you on the head with a waffle iron.

JERRY: We don't have a waffle iron.

ALISON: Lucky for you.

JERRY: I'll count it among my blessings.

ALISON: Everything's an argument, everything's an argument, everything's an argument.

JERRY: Would you like me to argue that?

ALISON: Say "*I love you*".

JERRY: Alison.

ALISON: Say it.

JERRY: When we say "*I love you*" we build a cage.

ALISON: You used to say it.

JERRY: I used to build cages.

ALISON: (*Sighs.*)

JERRY: You know how I feel.

ALISON: Drink your juice.

JERRY: Did you read the new draft?

ALISON: Of?

JERRY: Of the screenplay.

ALISON: Oh. I didn't yet no.

JERRY:	I thought you were going to show it to some people. Or—don't feel obligated.I mean if you think it has potential. But if it's no good just be honest.
ALISON:	It's good.
JERRY:	If you don't want to show it to anybody—
ALISON:	I will.
JERRY:	I mean why not explore connections you know.
ALISON:	I know.
JERRY:	If it's any good.
ALISON:	It is.
JERRY:	Or...
ALISON:	I will. Drink your juice.
JERRY:	I don't like beet juice.
ALISON:	You're not supposed to like beet juice you're supposed to like Scotch.
JERRY:	I'm on a fast.
ALISON:	It's good for you.
JERRY:	I'm on a fast!
ALISON:	Are you having an affair?
JERRY:	I thought we were talking about beet juice.
ALISON:	I know but are you?
JERRY:	God Alison. Your hormones must be...
ALISON:	Are you?
JERRY:	With whom?
ALISON:	I don't know... Some woman you met somewhere... Some patient.

JERRY: Yes I'm having an affair with a patient. I was going to wait until she got off crack and left her pimp before I told you about it. Jesus Alison.

ALISON: I'm sorry.

JERRY: I love you okay?

ALISON: Oh don't say it like that.

JERRY: Like what?

ALISON: You're just saying it because I'm an idiot.

JERRY: You're not an idiot.

ALISON: I don't know what's wrong with me.

JERRY: You're pregnant it's normal.

ALISON: Is it?

JERRY: Yes.

ALISON: Oh God. I'm sorry. I think I'm close to losing my mind.

JERRY: I wouldn't worry about it. *(Beat.)* Close only counts in horse shoes and handgrenades.

ALISON: And elevators.

JERRY: Have a nap. I'll call you later.

ALISON: Okay. Yeah. I'll be better later.

JERRY: Bye.

                JERRY leaves.

ALISON: Bye.

                ALISON watches him go. She looks out at the Audience.

                And I remember this was Monday because it was the first day of the twenty-first week. I counted in weeks because nine months seemed so much longer than forty weeks. Forty Mondays and this was twenty-one. The twenty-first week, the twenty-first Monday.

ALISON slowly pours the beet juice onto the ground as she speaks.

After twenty-one comes... Eighteen, nineteen, twenty, twenty-one. Twenty-one. Twenty-one. Eighteen, nineteen, twenty, twenty-one. After twenty-one. Twenty-one. After twenty-one we stop. We stop counting after twenty-one.

ALISON drops the glass. RICHARD appears. Silence.

RICHARD: It's nice out. It's almost hot. But not in a bad way.

A beat.

Apparently it's warmer than it's been for ages. For this time of year. It's a record or something. I mean it should be, you know, much colder.

A beat.

I'm not complaining.

A beat.

Hey, I haven't had a cigarette in three days! How about that? It's not even that hard. They say after three days all the nicotine is out of your system. Maybe this is as bad as it gets. Right? Maybe? Don't count on it. Right?

A beat.

But it's working. I've got a method this time. The No Method Method. No patches, no hypnotism, no nothing, just cold turkey. Which is a very specific kind of mindset. I was thinking I could get a kind of package together and start doing seminars. Cause it's working for me, it could work for other people right?

A beat.

You set your mind to it. You change yourself or whatever.

A beat.

I'm not eating more either. I'm just not really sure what to do with my hands. They say you're supposed to start doing something. To replace the smoking? A hobby or something. Maybe I should take up stamp collecting. Or ship building. Or bowling. Ha ha bowling. Didn't we used to go bowling? A few times. In university. Get high and go bowling or something.

ALISON: What's it like out?

RICHARD: It's nice.

ALISON: I hate that word.

RICHARD: It's pleasant.

ALISON: I'm so tired.

RICHARD: Should I go?

ALISON: When I was a kid—after my Dad left, sometimes my Mom would get so drunk my aunt would take me for a few days. My aunt lived in the suburbs, and as a treat what she'd do is take me to one of those big malls—with the pastel people and the plastic food places and the stores for everything and escalators for days. And what I used to do was go up to those big maps—those illuminated floor plans that had the little green dot that told you where you were. And I would stand there and stare at the little green dot that was supposed to be me, where I was, and I would get this…be filled with this sense of… That someone was watching, that someone was in charge. And if someone was watching, if someone was in charge, then maybe whoever they were might understand how I felt. But there isn't. And they don't.

RICHARD: I understand how you feel.

ALISON: How do I feel?

RICHARD: Filled with rage. So tired you can't lift your head off the pillow but filled with rage. Like what quicksand feels like. What it feels like to be quicksand. Big and angry and deep and empty. Like if someone stood over you they'd sink down and never get out.

            ALISON looks at RICHARD.

            But you'll feel better later. You will.

ALISON: Then why can't it be later? Why does it have to be now? Why do we have to be here?

RICHARD: We don't.

            RICHARD turns and addresses the Audience.

RICHARD: We're going to take a little break now.

            The house lights slowly come up as RICHARD exits.

ALISON: *(Calling after RICHARD.)* Richard! Thank you. *(To the Audience.)* Let's have a little break. Everything's going to be okay. Let's all have a break, have a drink.*(Exiting.)* I'll see you in a little while. Everything's going to be fine. Do you think I could have a drink, just a little—a glass of—

            ALISON is gone. The stage is empty.

            End of Act One.

Act Two

Lights fade up. Several moments pass. ALISON finally enters laughing. She is drinking a glass of wine.

ALISON: Don't believe what you hear about time when people say that time is against us because time is in fact, yes, our friend. Time passes and with it takes everything. And we start over, it's all new again, the first time, we can forget, we can feel better, we can be in love again, anything. It's going to work this time. From here on. It is. Everything's going to be great. It really is. Come on, let's go somewhere. Let's get out of here and go somewhere and do something fun. Let's just go out and get drunk or something.

JERRY appears.

JERRY: Getting drunk's not that much fun.

ALISON: Let's go out.

JERRY: I can't. I can't see people. It just reminds me how stuck I am. I'm so stuck.

ALISON: Jerry you're not. How?

JERRY: Every day I see my clients… Clients, that's a joke! It implies I perform some service. Every day, I see them, I talk to them and they're not going to get any better. They're not. And that's supposed to be okay. That's how the system works. I'm working maintenance. I'm a maintenance man. I might as well be working in a fucking factory.

ALISON: I read the new draft. I read it this morning.

JERRY: Whatever.

ALISON: It's going to be something Jerry, we're going to do it right.

JERRY: It's stupid to even think we can do this.

ALISON: Jerry? *"A long journey starts with a single step".*

JERRY: For Christ's sake Alison.

ALISON: Jerry? Look at me. Jerry? We'll be happy. We'll get what we want and we'll be happy.

JERRY: I...

ALISON: Jerry? You want to make this movie?

JERRY: It's ridiculous.

ALISON: Jerry?

JERRY: Yes.

ALISON: Would that make you happy?

JERRY: Yes.

ALISON: I'll make you happy.

              JERRY disappears while THOMAS appears. He is holding a script.

ALISON: So you've read the script?

THOMAS: Yes, thank you.

              THOMAS hands the script to ALISON. A beat. She takes it.

ALISON: He's working on another draft right now.

THOMAS: Is that an apology or a warning?

ALISON: Pardon me?

THOMAS: He does what your husband?

ALISON: He's a psychologist at a hospital, he has mostly
                 outpatients; a lot of people with drug problems,
                 criminal records. The Clayton character is a
                 composite of a few of people he's worked with.

                 *ALISON approaches THOMAS and opens the script
                 for him, flipping through it, looking for a scene,
                 eventually handing it off to him.*

                 I think it's good. The characters are very real.
                 Sondra needs a little work but she's coming along
                 nicely in the new draft. The weakness really is in the
                 structure but that's fixable.

THOMAS: Everything is fixable.

ALISON: At the same time there's something fresh about the
                 flawed structure.

THOMAS: Everything is fixable.

                 *THOMAS hands the script back to ALISON. A beat.
                 She takes it.*

ALISON: For Clayton I'm thinking an unknown—someone
                 maybe without a lot of training. Someone real.
                 Which means for Sondra we'd need a name.

THOMAS: Mmm.

ALISON: What do you think of the title?

THOMAS: What is it called again?

ALISON: *The Centre of the Universe.*

THOMAS: I don't know. Pretentious certainly.

ALISON: It's Clayton's perspective.

THOMAS: Mmm.

ALISON: So what do you think?

THOMAS: About what?

ALISON: The script.

THOMAS: Very North American.

ALISON: In what way?

THOMAS: In the way that it is exclusively concerned with itself
               but rationalizes its self-centeredness as an
               expression of the familiar; as *"sharing"*. It
               fundamentally lacks the conviction of its own self
               involvement.

ALISON: Oh. Where do you see that?

               *THOMAS takes the script from ALISON and flips
               through it.*

THOMAS: Scene 2. Scene 3. Scene 7. Scene 15. Scene 16. Scene
               20. Scene 21. Scene—

               ALISON moves to take the script.

ALISON: Fine.

               THOMAS walks away with the script.

THOMAS: For example. In Scene 22, in the graveyard, Clayton
               spends an entire page detailing the events of his life
               for Sondra and when she says *"What a remarkable
               life."* Clayton responds: *"But just a life like any life."*
               What is this? If it's no different than any life then
               why waste my time with it? If it's already my life
               then there's nothing to tell me.

ALISON: But he goes on to say... But... Clayton's just—
               Jerry's just pointing out— We can all identify with
               his struggle.

THOMAS: Bullshit. Jerry's saying *"But just a life like any life."*

ALISON: I'm sure he's not married to the line, he can change
               it.

THOMAS: It is not the line! It is the mind behind the line.
               This... This...feigned belief in universality. This

mortal fear of exclusivity. Bullshit. What is interesting, what is dramatic is "*I*" and "*Now*" not how alike we are and how this has always been the way. No particular offense to your husband, this is the problem with most screenwriting these days.

ALISON: I guess that explains it then.

THOMAS: What?

ALISON: Why you haven't made a film in five years.

ALISON takes the script from THOMAS.

THOMAS: Who are you talking to about producing?

ALISON: I'm producing.

THOMAS: You?

ALISON: I want to see this film get made.

THOMAS: There's more to it than that.

ALISON: And I'm organized and I can use a telephone.

THOMAS: But we're not joking now.

ALISON: And I am owed many favours by many people.

THOMAS: Are you trying to save your marriage?

ALISON: Pardon me?

THOMAS: I just wonder— Such a sacrifice?

ALISON: I want to make something.

THOMAS: For your husband?

ALISON: And myself.

THOMAS: All right. Let's set up a meeting with the writer.

ALISON: He'll have the new draft by Friday.

THOMAS: Good.

ALISON: But… And…

THOMAS: Yes?

ALISON: Can you get Diane Drake?

THOMAS: Ah, perhaps there is a producer in there.

>*THOMAS disappears. The FIRST ASSISTANT DIRECTOR enters wearing a headset and carrying a script. As she passes ALISON she hands ALISON the script and takes ALISON's glass of wine. As the FIRST AD takes ALISON's wine ALISON reaches to keep it and in the process drops the script which scatters across the floor. Through the scene ALISON scrambles to gather the pages.*

FIRST AD: *(Into headset.)* Apparently she left the hotel.…I don't know when…They're lit… Yes they're lit now… We could go to an exterior… It's not my call… That's a producer call… Yes there is… Right in front of me… What?… I'm losing you… Hello? Hello?… *(Exiting.)* Batteries!

>*PAUL enters wearing a makeup apron and carries a script.*

PAUL: Alison? I've got some problems with this scene.

ALISON: Which scene Paul?

PAUL: The one with Clayton in the church with the prostitute.

>*DIANE DRAKE crosses the stage.*

DIANE: Morning.

ALISON: Diane the call was for eight thirty.

DIANE: I told Jennie I'd be late.

>*DIANE exits. The FIRST AD crosses the stage rushing after DIANE.*

ALISON: Who's Jennie?

PAUL: 64A.

ALISON: Who's Jennie?

FIRST AD: Assistant wardrobe.

ALISON: She called the wardrobe assistant to tell her she'd be
             late?

             The FIRST AD exits.

PAUL: Scene 64A.

ALISON: What?

PAUL: 64A with Clayton and the prostitute in the church?

ALISON: Right okay what?

PAUL: Does it have to be in a church?

ALISON: Yes. That's the location.

PAUL: I don't want to be disrespectful.

ALISON: Pardon me?

PAUL: Can't it be in a park or something.

ALISON: In a park.

PAUL: Instead of a church. I don't want to be disrespectful.

ALISON: To whom?

PAUL: To God.

ALISON: God doesn't care.

             The FIRST AD enters.

FIRST AD: Hair says this day has already been established but
             that's not what I've got in my notes.

PAUL: God cares.

ALISON:	*(To AD.)* What day is it?
FIRST AD:	Day 13. Church and exterior.
PAUL:	We could do it outside the church even.
ALISON:	*(To AD.)* What do Hair's notes say?
FIRST AD:	Hair doesn't have his notes.
ALISON:	Then how does Hair know?
FIRST AD:	That's what I said!

The FIRST AD exits.

PAUL:	I wouldn't mind if it was outside the church.
ALISON:	Paul there are twenty-five people in the church right now who have been lighting it for the last three hours.
PAUL:	It's just I prayed on it last night and I don't have a good feeling about it.
ALISON:	The scene was always set in a church Paul.
PAUL:	I only prayed on it last night.
ALISON:	Maybe you should have prayed on it before.
PAUL:	I'm just trying to tell you how I feel.

The FIRST AD enters.

FIRST AD:	Hair says he needs two hours with Diane.
ALISON:	Well tell Hair… For Christ's sake!

The FIRST AD exits.

PAUL:	Do you pray Alison?
ALISON:	Not lately.
PAUL:	It doesn't matter what you believe. You can still pray. It's just about taking a quiet moment to

consider what's important. Maybe we should pray together right now.

ALISON: Fuck off Paul. Please.

PAUL: I don't have a good feeling about this Alison.

PAUL exits. THOMAS enters.

THOMAS: We're lit. The light itself is lit. Can we get something happening here?

ALISON: Diane just arrived and apparently Hair needs two hours with her which can't happen but I can't talk to Hair because Hair won't talk to me because apparently I'm shrill with him and now Paul has some kind of spiritual crisis about getting a blow job in a church.

THOMAS: Ah, it was ridiculous to set that scene in a church.

ALISON: What?

THOMAS: Another bald metaphor.

ALISON: Well... But the church is lit.

PAUL enters.

PAUL: Oh hey Thomas, listen I want to talk to you about this scene.

THOMAS: In the church?

PAUL: Yeah, see I'm a Christian and—

THOMAS: Yeah I know.

PAUL: Oh yeah?

THOMAS: Yes it's why you were cast in the role.

PAUL: Oh.

THOMAS: And this scene... What number is this scene?

PAUL:	64.
THOMAS:	64.
PAUL:	64A.
THOMAS:	And how many scenes in the script.
PAUL:	Uh…
THOMAS:	One hundred and twenty two. This scene 64, at the almost exact centre of the script—of the story—to remind us that God is at the centre of life—at the centre of the universe.
PAUL:	Oh.
THOMAS:	Good writing huh? When it knows more than we do.
PAUL:	Yeah.
THOMAS:	Bye bye.
PAUL:	Bye.
THOMAS:	Bye bye.

THOMAS sends PAUL on his way.

ALISON:	*(To THOMAS.)* Thanks.
THOMAS:	And you are shrill with Hair.
ALISON:	I know.
THOMAS:	In my many years in film you know the one thing I've learned? A few flowers never hurt a hairdresser.
ALISON:	Okay.
THOMAS:	Looks to me you could use a few flowers yourself.

JERRY enters holding a donut. As ALISON talks to JERRY she manages to gather up the last of the script pages.

JERRY:	Hey!
ALISON:	Hi.
THOMAS:	*(To JERRY.)* We need to talk about the script.
JERRY:	Is there a problem?
THOMAS:	*(Exiting.)* We need to talk about the script.
JERRY:	*(To ALISON.)* Again?
ALISON:	Oh he's a director, directors always want to talk about the script.
JERRY:	How's it going?
ALISON:	Great!
JERRY:	It's really exciting isn't it.
ALISON:	Yeah.
JERRY:	Listen I'm sure you're really busy but I was just at the food table thing?
ALISON:	Craft services.
JERRY:	Yeah, and the donuts were really stale.
ALISON:	Oh. Okay. Well I'll get somebody to get somebody on that.
JERRY:	It would probably be a good thing. For morale you know.
ALISON:	Morale yes morale.
JERRY:	See you later.
ALISON:	See you later.

> *JERRY gives ALISON the donut and leaves. The AD crosses and takes ALISON's script. ALISON throws the donut after JERRY.*

RICHARD: It doesn't matter what you do it's going to happen the same way.

ALISON: What?

RICHARD throws a shawl at ALISON.

RICHARD: You still haven't learned to start a fire.

ALISON: There was nothing to burn.

RICHARD: There's two full cords of wood out back.

ALISON: I'd like to burn that goddamn film is what I'd like to burn.

RICHARD: You're getting ahead of yourself.

ALISON: What?

RICHARD: Some people liked the film.

ALISON: Who liked it?

RICHARD: Jerry says it's going to do well on video.

ALISON: Yeah in Thailand.

RICHARD: What's wrong with Thailand?

ALISON: Nothing forget it.

RICHARD: It's too bad Jerry couldn't come up this weekend.

ALISON: I didn't invite him. He's busy. He got a couple of story editing jobs.

RICHARD: See that's good. The movie got him some connections.

ALISON: Uh huh.

RICHARD: Connections. That's what it's all about. Before my Dad died he was always on me about making connections, he was right. He was right but he was wrong.

*ALISON watches RICHARD, she hears him in a
way she hasn't heard him before.*

Because it's not just the networking kind of
connections. It's the connections of everyone—of all
things—you know? And I was thinking: I don't
really feel very connected to anything really.
Sometimes lately when I'm here at the cottage I feel
like *"I like it here"* but I think a feeling of
connectedness is supposed to be more than just *"I
like it."* Do you know about Atman? It's a Hindu
thing. It's the eternal part of us that is beyond
physical description. It's like, something about *"that
which pervades all"*. Something about being the thing
and being the thing which experiences the thing and
the thing that understands that experience all at the
same time. It's pretty interesting. I'm thinking about
getting into Hinduism.

ALISON: That might be good for you.

*RICHARD does not hear ALISON because this is
not the way she answered him when they originally
had this conversation. He repeats himself until she
says the line she said.*

RICHARD: I'm thinking about getting into Hinduism.

ALISON: That might be a good thing for you to do.

RICHARD: I'm thinking about getting into Hinduism.

ALISON: I think it's a good idea to try something different.

RICHARD: I'm thinking about getting into Hinduism.

                 A beat.

ALISON: You'd never stick to it, you never stick to anything.

RICHARD: That's true.

                 *ALISON gazes out into the Audience through the
                 remainder of the scene.*

RICHARD: Do you want to sit outside?

ALISON: Not right now.

RICHARD: We'll take our drinks, I'll roll a joint, we'll sit on the porch.

ALISON: Not right now.

RICHARD: It's nice out.

ALISON: Fuck nice.

> *DIANE DRAKE enters drinking a glass of water and reading aloud from a magazine. ALISON sits silently looking away from the action.*

DIANE: *(Reading.)* "As a film The Centre of the Universe *owes more of a debt to Russ Meyer than Scorcese or DePalma."* Who's Russ Meyer?

RICHARD: Isn't he a British guy or...? Alison?

DIANE: Anyway. *(Reading.)* "The film sloshes along with former art house darling Thomas Roman at the rickety helm."* The helm. That's a ship thing isn't it.

RICHARD: Yeah I think so. Yeah it is.

DIANE: Ship metaphors are so boring. Blah blah blah.

> *JERRY enters with a bottle of wine and a glass for himself and one for RICHARD.*

JERRY: *(To ALISON.)* Do you want the salad dressed now?

DIANE: Who's Russ Meyer?

JERRY: An American director from the 60s and 70s.

DIANE: Is he good?

JERRY: He was a master of a certain kind of cinema.

> *JERRY hands RICHARD a glass and pours him some wine.*

DIANE: Well that's good!

RICHARD: It's a recommended rental. They gave it a recommended rental.

JERRY: They said it was unintentionally hilarious.

RICHARD: But they recommended it.

JERRY: *(To ALISON.)* Salad's done, you want it dressed?

                ALISON does not respond.

DIANE: No you see Robert the thing is—

RICHARD: Richard.

DIANE: What did I say?

RICHARD: Robert.

DIANE: No no I meant to say…

RICHARD: Richard.

DIANE: Yeah. No the thing about the film is it didn't work because it was too real and the people who needed to see it didn't see it because the people who did see it were to afraid of how real it was.

RICHARD: Uh huh. Yeah I kind of get that.

DIANE: Because the people who did see it were the goddamn critics. But here's to the life *The Centre of the Universe* deserves—which it will have now on video—because the people who need to see it will see it—unless the goddamn critics get in the way again. But more importantly here's to Jerry and many more future projects.

RICHARD: Hear hear. Cheers.

DIANE: Cheers. *(To JERRY.)* You really must write something else for me. Just something small. *(To RICHARD.)* He's such a wonderful writer—it's such a pleasure to speak his words.

RICHARD: *(To JERRY.)* Whoa. Hey.

DIANE: *(To JERRY.)* Cheers.

JERRY: Cheers.

RICHARD: *(To DIANE.)* So you're in town for a while?

DIANE: I just came in for the video launch and some meetings—and I have a naturopath here I like.

RICHARD: But you know I must say Diane you were great in the movie.

DIANE: Ahh you're sweet. Thanks it was fun. To bad about that little fellow, what was his name?

JERRY: Paul?

DIANE: Paul yeah, he was sweet but—not much presence really though did he.

ALISON: Some people thought he carried the movie.

DIANE: Carried it?

ALISON: Yes.

DIANE: *(Laughing.)* Carried it where? All the way to the video store.

JERRY: *(To ALISON.)* I didn't dress the salad. *(To RICHARD.)* And we're off meat again!

RICHARD: That's okay I'm trying to cut down.

DIANE: Could I… Another mineral water?

RICHARD: I'll get it.

JERRY: I'll help.

RICHARD and JERRY exit. A long pause.

DIANE: You know Alison it's strange—when I first met you you were just a journalist to me and I never imagine that journalists have, you know, lives. I mean it's like teachers. When I was in school and I'd bump into a teacher, say at the grocery store, I'd always be amazed that teachers you know ate or shopped or had families. It's as if they just disappeared when they weren't teaching, like they went into a frozen chamber or something. Like without me to teach they didn't exist. That's what journalists were always like to me.

> *Pause.*

But I guess it's different really—I mean in some ways without journalists I wouldn't exist.

> *Pause.*

I mean Diane Drake is a bit of an invention in a lot of ways. You know my real name isn't Drake. It's Briss. It's not even Diane. It's Bonnie. Bonnie Briss. Which loosely translates into "a happy ritualistic circumcision." It's the kind of name you kind of need to change if you're planning on seeing it in print. I mean anyway I haven't been Bonnie Briss since I was six or seven. I like Diane Drake better. It's not like there's a Bonnie Briss anyway. Or I wonder. Some little, you know, entity wandering around wondering where I am. Probably totally not.

ALISON: Probably totally not.

DIANE: Anyway. Are you all right?

ALISON: Probably totally not.

> *ALISON rises to pour herself some more wine. She stumbles slightly.*

DIANE: Maybe you should have some water.

ALISON: You're not drinking tonight Diane?

DIANE: I'm on a bit of a detox thing.

ALISON: A program.

DIANE: No! Just a...break. What a sweet little place you have.

ALISON: I'd give you the tour but Jerry just started ripping his office apart.

DIANE: Really? Why?

ALISON: A space thing. I thought we could move but he likes the house.

DIANE: Really. Yes it's cozy.

> *RICHARD and JERRY enter. JERRY gives DIANE a glass of soda.*

JERRY: *(To RICHARD.)* You've been saying that since you got out of University.

RICHARD: I am getting organized.

JERRY: You don't even wear a watch.

RICHARD: I don't like anything on my arms.

JERRY: Organized or not we are the image we project, projected back to us by the mirror of others. It's artificial.

RICHARD: All right all right.

JERRY: And all of these women—

RICHARD: *"These women,"* you make it sound like I'm some sort of Casanova.

DIANE: Which women?

ALISON: Richard's women.

RICHARD: All right Alison.

DIANE: What's he got, like a harem.

ALISON: Basically.

RICHARD   All right Alison.

ALISON: You're saying it's not like that?

RICHARD   No. Yes, no it isn't.

ALISON: Just in the past year! That girl from the bookstore, the girl from the phone thing—

RICHARD: Oh God...

DIANE: Do tell!

RICHARD: It wasn't a phone thing.

ALISON: It was the internet.

RICHARD   It was nothing.

ALISON: The lesbian.

RICHARD   She was bisexual.

ALISON: I liked her.

RICHARD: Alison...

ALISON: What was her name?

RICHARD   Peggy. We were just friends.

ALISON: *(To DIANE.)* *"Just friends"* to Richard means he doesn't have his own toothbrush at your place.

RICHARD: I didn't know you were keeping a list.

ALISON: A partial list.

RICHARD: And your point exactly is?

JERRY: What we were talking about was projection.

DIANE: Oh projection. That can be dangerous. I've had projection several times. Actors get it all the time.

ALISON: You don't *"get"* projection you experience projection.

DIANE: You can get it—I've had it.

ALISON: You can't *"have"* it.

DIANE: I know what I've had and I've had it.

ALISON: It's not a venereal disease.

DIANE: I beg your pardon.

JERRY: Hey it's just language—simple vibrations in the diaphragm.

ALISON: *(To JERRY.)* I thought language was all we had to go on.

JERRY: Nope—it's just a response to the idea of the self as an entity separate from the thing we call "me."

ALISON: Right.

DIANE: So Jerry, I hear you're doing some renovating.

JERRY: Well not renovating really—

ALISON: I would call putting in a window renovating.

DIANE: Show me. I'm thinking about doing some work on my place.

JERRY: Sure but...are we ready to eat?

ALISON: Go ahead.

JERRY: Okay. Come on.

DIANE: Great.

          JERRY and DIANE exit.

RICHARD: Hey what's your problem cool down. You're so giving me a hard time in front of her. And you never liked Peggy at all.

RICHARD pours himself and ALISON more wine. ALISON steps forward and looks out into the Audience as if waiting for something. RICHARD takes out a vial and snorts some powder off his hand as he speaks.

Did I offend her? I think I offended her. Do you think she likes me? She intimidates me, she's so...translucent. You know? I'm all clammy. Are you clammy? I'm so clammy. You know this morning I couldn't decide between a shower and a bath. So I smoked a joint and I thought about it and I thought you know I prefer showers but maybe baths are better for me. You know soaking the body as opposed to just running water over it. But maybe I don't want to feel my body as intensely as I would in a bath—like I live my life so much outside my body that a shower is preferable—you know just a comma of awareness as opposed to a whole sentence of awareness. Which is maybe all about how much I hate myself. So I didn't take either—a shower or a bath. I think I smoke too much dope. Do you think I offended her? Alison? I'm so clammy. Alison? What are you doing?

ALISON: Waiting.

RICHARD: For what?

ALISON: Waiting. Waiting.

DIANE enters followed by JERRY.

DIANE: I have to go.

RICHARD: Huh?

JERRY: Diane.

DIANE exits briefly and returns with her coat.

RICHARD: What's going on?

JERRY: Nothing.

DIANE: This was a mistake.

RICHARD: Are you okay?

DIANE: I have to go.

JERRY: Now. Look.

RICHARD: I'll give you a lift.

DIANE: No. Thank you.

JERRY: Stay.

DIANE: Do you want me to stay?

RICHARD: Of course.

DIANE: I'm asking Jerry. Do you want me to stay Jerry?

JERRY: Yes.

DIANE: All right I'll stay. I'll stay because I have something to say.

RICHARD: What?

DIANE: I'm pregnant.

RICHARD: Huh?

> *JERRY and DIANE exit. RICHARD leaves passing behind ALISON.*

ALISON: *(To the Audience.)* Retrospect is everything… It is the road ahead of you and the horizon behind you. In retrospect it all comes together. All the little details turn into that road map you didn't know you'd been following all this time. All this long time. And in retrospect we look back to see how we got there. What it must have been that got us there, how it must have happened.

> *DIANE appears on the other side of the stage. She drinks coffee from a styrofoam cup and nibbles on a donut. Soon JERRY joins her. ALISON watches them.*

JERRY: Hi there.

DIANE: Oh gosh hey, hi there.

JERRY: Jerry.

DIANE: No I know. I'm Diane.

JERRY: No hey I know. Hi.

DIANE: Hi. Listen I'm just so thrilled to meet you.

JERRY: Oh yeah?

DIANE: I thought I'd meet you in LA at the reading.

JERRY: Yeah no I have a…other job.

DIANE: No I know yeah, you're a psychiatrist.

JERRY: Yeah. A…well, a psychologist. I thought a Ph.D. would be more challenging than Med School.

DIANE: Right. Well whatever you are you're great at it. The script is brilliant. You really understand people.

JERRY: Really, well.

DIANE: The situation's so real. The characters are so authentic.

JERRY: Yeah?

DIANE: I read so much crap. Jerry? I read so much crap? An actor is so grateful for this kind of writing.

JERRY: Well I've really loved your work that I've seen you do.

DIANE: I don't want to talk about me.

JERRY: Oh… I…

DIANE: No I'm sorry. I don't mean to be whatever but really I want to talk about your script. I can't believe you haven't written before.

JERRY: I've written—you know stories and—

DIANE: You're born to write film. Really. And you got this together on your own!

JERRY: Yeah, no well, it was my wife really who pulled all this together, pulled in favours, you know, got it going.

DIANE: Your wife?

JERRY: Alison?

DIANE: Oh Alison right right Alison right. Oh you guys are married oh. She's sweet. I know Alison.

JERRY: Yeah.

DIANE: I was married once. For about ten minutes. I was a bit much for him I guess.

JERRY: Yeah. I mean you seem independent.

DIANE: Do I?

JERRY: Yeah.

DIANE: Looks are deceiving aren't they.

JERRY: I've heard that.

DIANE: Do you have any kids?

JERRY: Oh. No. I'm sorry. Uh.

DIANE: What?

JERRY: Just uh. My wife...Alison last year she miscarried...Or well it was almost full term so...

DIANE: Oh gosh I'm so sorry. It must be terrible.

JERRY: It's been really difficult for her. I can't...even myself really, even imagine what it must be like. For me it was still a kind of abstraction, the whole notion or the possibility of a child.

DIANE:	Uh huh.
JERRY:	But for her it was…well…real.
DIANE:	Uh huh.
JERRY:	But it's forced me to be more…fatalistic. Not in the sense of… Not so much with the Calvinistic implications of the idea.
DIANE:	Uh huh uh huh.
JERRY:	Perhaps it's just simplistic rationalization; to buffer the pain.
DIANE:	Uh huh. No, you know I was up for something once where that was the situation. That I would have had to play? And when I was preparing I went there? And it was just… What a terrible terrible…I'm sorry…I'm such a sap…I'm sorry.
JERRY:	No. Yes. It's a very emotional thing.
DIANE:	You can't even look at me sideways and I start to cry.
JERRY:	It must be difficult.
DIANE:	Well… You know…
JERRY:	But a wonderful gift as well. To be so responsive.
DIANE:	Yeah. Well thanks. Yeah.
JERRY:	I wish my patients could be so connected. But I guess if they were they wouldn't be my patients would they? Put me out of a job.
DIANE:	You've got a new job now.
JERRY:	Thank you.
DIANE:	Can I give you a hug?
JERRY:	Uh. Sure.

DIANE hugs JERRY.

DIANE: Thanks.

JERRY: Yeah. No. Thanks.

DIANE: Anyway.

JERRY: Anyway.

DIANE: I am so late.

JERRY: Ah they're always behind.

DIANE: Exactly.

JERRY: Can I get you something?

DIANE: I should go.

DIANE gives JERRY her donut.

DIANE: But could you take this, it is so stale? I don't really mind myself it's just the crew, it's important to keep the morale up.

JERRY: I'm with you there.

DIANE exit. JERRY watches her go then exits.

ALISON: And sometimes it's much worse then you imagined.

THOMAS appears. He wears a dressing gown and carries two glasses of champagne.

THOMAS: What are you saying darling?

ALISON: Never mind.

THOMAS gives ALISON a glass of champagne. He watches her.

ALISON: What?

THOMAS: I could get used to this.

ALISON: To what?

THOMAS:	Contentment.
ALISON:	Oh you'd just get tired of contentment soon enough and be back to insignificance.
THOMAS:	You are a fascinating woman.
ALISON:	No I'm a woman who got hurt and instead of getting angry tried to get mellow—but not having the metabolism for mellow she just got cold.
THOMAS:	You weren't so cold a few minutes ago.
ALISON:	I know when to turn it on and off. I'm like a tap.
THOMAS:	Let's go somewhere tonight.
ALISON:	I'm working tonight.
THOMAS:	What can a person possibly write about a party?
ALISON:	People do it all the time.
THOMAS:	And for what?
ALISON:	Five dollars and fifty cents a word.
THOMAS:	Yes well this is America.
ALISON:	No. This is a hotel room. And as I remember King of the Gypsies it was my credit card we left at the desk.
THOMAS:	Do you need money?
ALISON:	Everybody needs money.
THOMAS:	Don't go yet.
ALISON:	What Thomas?
THOMAS:	Come and live with me a while in Italy, let me take care of you.
ALISON:	*(Turning away.)* I don't want to be taken care of Thomas. Look you're a nice guy, you come into town once in a while, we get together. Let's not turn it into something it isn't.

A beat.

THOMAS: You know the scene from Hector Finch? The scene with the couple on the bridge with the flower? The thing with the flower?

ALISON: What?

THOMAS: It was Diane's idea—she improvised it—I had no idea until it happened. All of it, the tearing, the pocket, the river. It was all Diane. She was playing, she was being silly. Just know she has some good in her. Don't hate her so much. It hurts you.

THOMAS disappears.

ALISON: It's not her I hate.

The light shifts. JUSTIN appears. He stands behind ALISON, presenting her with a full glass of wine. He is a young street-wise punk. Eventually he starts kissing her neck and shoulders as he speaks.

JUSTIN: Who do you hate?

ALISON: Why?

JUSTIN: Cause I'll take care of whoever it is.

ALISON: You will will you?

JUSTIN: Or I can get somebody to. I got lots of friends.

ALISON: I bet you do.

JUSTIN: You know it.

ALISON: Connie Hoy.

JUSTIN: That's who you hate?

ALISON: Yes. And her perfect little house and her perfect little family.

JUSTIN: She got a dog? I know a guy who could take care of it.

ALISON:	Can't we just give her cancer or something?
JUSTIN:	We can do anything. We got the power to do anything to all the fuckers of the world. Nobody should be mean to you. You're special.
ALISON:	Am I?
JUSTIN:	You're beautiful.
ALISON:	What's your name again?
JUSTIN:	Justin.
ALISON:	Just in case. Just in time. This just in.
JUSTIN:	You know it. Mmmmm you smell nice.
ALISON:	Who do you know here Justin?
JUSTIN:	Everybody.
ALISON:	You don't know me.
JUSTIN:	But I will. Won't I?
ALISON:	I think you will.
JUSTIN:	You wanna get high?

> *JUSTIN takes out a small bag of white powder which he deftly empties and snorts off the back of his hand.*

ALISON:	I want to get drunk.
JUSTIN:	You already are drunk.
ALISON:	Then I want to stay drunk.
JUSTIN:	That can be arranged.
ALISON:	Good.
JUSTIN:	You got someplace we can go?
ALISON:	Yeah.

JUSTIN: I like to deal with finances up front. If you don't mind.

            ALISON considers this a moment.

ALISON: No I don't mind.

            JUSTIN kisses her. She pulls away and drinks down her glass of wine. She hands the glass to JUSTIN and he leaves with it. Light shifts. ALISON looks out at the Audience, all seems unfamiliar to her. She slowly sinks to the floor. JUSTIN reappears with a full glass of wine which he places on the floor beside ALISON.

JUSTIN: It's fucking Steven Spielberg.

            JERRY enters. ALISON remains seated on the floor.

JERRY: *(To JUSTIN.)* Shouldn't you be somewhere? Like in jail?

JUSTIN: Shouldn't you fuck off.

JERRY: Charming.

JUSTIN: Fuck you fuck.

JERRY: Could you maybe say one sentence without *"fuck"* in it?

JUSTIN: I don't talk in fucking *"sentences"*. Faggot

JERRY: Is he living here? Have you got this little prick living here?

JUSTIN: Hey! You want a fucking smack? Hey!

ALISON: Justin! Go! Go!

            JUSTIN exits.

JERRY: Jesus Alison.

ALISON: What?

JERRY: What is this?

ALISON: What is what?

JERRY: What are you doing?

ALISON: Thinking.

JERRY: Do you know what he does for a living?

ALISON: He's helping me with my schedule.

JERRY: He's a gigolo.

ALISON: *(Getting up off the floor.)* Oh Jerry, update your thesaurus.

JERRY: I'm not paying his way.

ALISON: You're not paying anybody's way you son of a bitch.

JERRY: Is that so? Then why am I here?

ALISON: I don't know.

JERRY: What was so urgent you had to see me?

ALISON: Oh right. Oh right oh right. I just need a little loan. A little one.

JERRY: We still owe money on the movie.

ALISON: I thought it was number one in Japan or something.

JERRY: It's the number eight rental in Thailand and we still owe money on it.

ALISON: Okay but this is just short term.

JERRY: You don't look so good Alison.

ALISON: Exactly, which is why I need a little loan to get it together you know.

JERRY: How much?

ALISON: Ten thousand.

JERRY: What?!

ALISON: Five thousand.

JERRY: Christ Alison.

ALISON: Two thousand.

JERRY: Give me a couple of days.

            JERRY looks at ALISON a moment.

            I think you need to slow down a bit.

ALISON: Exactly I know I do exactly.

JERRY: And listen Alison, I want to tell you this before you hear it from someone else. Diane and I are separating. It mutual. It's the best thing. And she's going to take Rebecca—which is best. Diane will have the house and Rebecca's starting school next year so, I think it's best that it be this way.

            JERRY leaves. RICHARD enters carrying a sad little birthday cake lit with four candles. JUSTIN enters behind, dressed to go out. He carries a bottle of wine with which he refills ALISON's glass.

RICHARD: *(Singing to the tune of "Happy Birthday".) "I hate this song/I hate this song/I really love you/But I hate this song."*

ALISON: Oh wow.

JUSTIN: What the fuck's that? What's wrong with the song?

            ALISON blows out the candles.

RICHARD: Sorry.

JUSTIN: It's a good fucking song.

ALISON: I blew out all the candles.

JUSTIN: It's not even her fucking birthday.

ALISON: What?

JUSTIN: Her birthday's tomorrow. It's only fucking ten
            o'clock.

ALISON: Richard! It's not even my birthday yet! I blew out
            my candles and everything. Is that bad luck? Is that
            bad luck?

JUSTIN: No shut up. You just might not get your wish that's
            all.

ALISON: Oh no! I forgot to wish!

JUSTIN: That's good then, you'll wish tomorrow when it's
            really your birthday. Fuck.

RICHARD: Sorry I just thought…we were already celebrating
            you know. I made it myself.

ALISON: Awww, thanks.

            JUSTIN cuts himself a piece of cake and takes a bite.

RICHARD: *(To ALISON.)* Are you going to make any
            resolutions?

JUSTIN: That's fucking New Year's.

RICHARD: No but you can make a resolution anytime.

JUSTIN: Yeah I made a resolution. No more of your fucking
            cake.

            JUSTIN throws his piece back on the cake.

JUSTIN: We gotta go soon Al.

RICHARD: I was thinking about making a resolution.

ALISON: Oh yeah.

JUSTIN: We gotta go soon Al.

ALISON: We gotta go soon Richard.

RICHARD: Where?

ALISON: *(To JUSTIN.)* Where?

JUSTIN: We got two parties baby. That movie thing and something at 1:30.

ALISON: *(Sitting on the floor.)* One thirty. That's so late.

JUSTIN: It'll be fun.

RICHARD   What is it? I'll come.

JUSTIN: It's work.

RICHARD   You're going.

JUSTIN: I'm her assistant.

RICHARD   Oh.

JUSTIN: We gotta go soon Al.

RICHARD: *(Sitting on the floor beside ALISON.)* I was thinking about making a resolution. Alison?

JUSTIN: Are you going to do something with your hair?

ALISON: Oh I know I know.

JUSTIN: It's a fucking mess.

ALISON: I know. I need my hat.

JUSTIN: Which hat?

ALISON: Witch Hat? Fucking *"Witch Hat"* what?

JUSTIN: Which of your many fucking hats do you want?

              JUSTIN exits to get ALISON a hat.

ALISON: *(Calling after JUSTIN.)* The...the one...the other one...

RICHARD: Guess who died.

ALISON: Oh no. Who?

                 *As he speaks RICHARD fumbles through a series of
                 little plastic dope packages in his pocket, all of them
                 empty.*

RICHARD: Connie Hoy. Cancer. She and Steeves were still
                 together. Three kids. This is last year or something.
                 She was sick for a while I guess. I mean I saw her at
                 the airport a couple of years ago and she seemed
                 fine. She seemed happy.

ALISON: Nobody's happy.

RICHARD: No. But she seemed fine. It can just happen like that.
                 The world can just end. But it does all the time. The
                 world ended lots of times. The Permian Age. Ever
                 hear of the Permian Age? 250 million years ago
                 ninty-five percent of the world's species were
                 wiped out. Happens all the time. Some little species
                 is just walking along or swimming along and then
                 just like that. Over. The Connie Hoy Age ended. The
                 world ends every time. The Richard Age. The
                 Alison Age. I was thinking about making a
                 resolution. I was thinking of maybe cleaning up a
                 bit. I'm feeling kind of sick all the time. Maybe we
                 could clean up together.

ALISON: Clean up what?

RICHARD: I don't know. Nothing.

                 *JUSTIN re-enters with a cardboard box. He drops it
                 near ALISON.*

JUSTIN: Here pick a fucking hat.

                 *ALISON goes through the box pulling out hats,
                 books, a walkman, speakers, gloves, more hats.*

JUSTIN: Richard buddy we gotta go.

RICHARD: *(Rising.)* Okay. Yeah okay.

JUSTIN: See you later.

RICHARD   Can I get a bag off you?

JUSTIN: No problem. Fifty bucks.

RICHARD   I haven't got any cash.

> *JUSTIN produces two small plastic bags from his pocket.*

JUSTIN: Owe me. Here owe me for two.

RICHARD: Yeah great thanks.

> *RICHARD moves to leave.*

RICHARD: I'll see you later. Happy birthday Alison.

ALISON: Yeah happy birthday.

JUSTIN: See ya later. Thanks for the cake.

RICHARD: Yeah thanks.

> *RICHARD leaves.*

JUSTIN: Did you find a fucking hat yet?

> *At the bottom of the box ALISON comes across her bottle of sand. She takes it out and hugs it to her.*

ALISON: Look! Oh look!

JUSTIN: Oh Christ.

ALISON: Look.

JUSTIN: Yeah whatever we gotta go.

ALISON: Feel it! It's warm! It's still warm like the desert!

JUSTIN: No it's warm like the fucking radiator it was sitting on.

> *ALISON curls up on the floor with the bottle.*

JUSTIN: Look I'm going, I got some deliveries to make. Are you coming?

ALISON: We killed Connie Hoy.

JUSTIN: What?

ALISON: We killed her.

JUSTIN: Who?

ALISON: Connie Hoy.

JUSTIN: Who the fuck's that?

ALISON: We killed her.

JUSTIN: Jesus I'm going. Get a fucking grip lady.

JUSTIN leaves.

ALISON: It's still warm... Happy birthday to me... Happy birthday to me...I'm sorry...I'm sorry.

The light slowly shifts, growing dim. ALISON lies on the floor, mumbling to herself. We begin to hear the following recorded text. Slowly ALISON sits up and listens.

VOICE: You have reached an automated messaging service: *(ALISON and JUSTIN's voices:)* Everybody!

VOICE: ...Cannot take your call at this time. Please leave a brief message at the sound of the tone and your message will be promptly returned.

RICHARD's
VOICE: *(Drunkenly.)* Alison? I was thinking. I was thinking about all the reasons of life. Of my life and everybody's life. All the reasons. And the ones I thought of, they weren't really reasons, and then the ones I did think of were all reasons of power and bullshit reasons—like my father, exactly like my father. He was right. Fuck. I never did anything. *(Pause.)* You know how I don't like stuff on my

arms? I was thinking it was because of me—because of maybe me in another life in some kind of prison with handcuffs or ropes or something. I wonder where I'll go now. They say that about necks. If you've been hung. In my next life maybe I'll never wear a tie. I never fucking wore a tie in this one. I'm sorry Alison. I'm sorry. I love you. Bye.

ALISON is now standing, facing the Audience. From her pocket she takes out the folded paper we saw earlier. She opens it and begins to read it to us.

ALISON: (*Reading.*) If you try you can feel the walls—of this bubble, this shell we breathe around ourselves, this tiny room we live in all our lives. This tiny room filled with mirrors and barely room to move. And then one day something happens—something happens and you see where you are and you leave the room and you go out into the world and you realize we've all been so alone, locked in our bubbles, our shells, our tiny rooms, all so alone, all this time.

ALISON folds up the paper and puts it away.

I wrote that. It needs an ending but I can't seem to find one.

ALISON turns and faces upstage where a WAITER is setting up a table and two chairs for lunch. DIANE appears and the WAITER seats her. They speak quietly.

WAITER: May I bring you something to drink while you're waiting for your friend?

DIANE: Yes, a class of sparkling water, no ice. And you can bring me a small market salad. I'll order an entree when—

WAITER: When your friend arrives.

DIANE: Yes. I'll keep the menu.

WAITER: Would you like some bread?

DIANE: No that's fine just the salad.

> ALISON *enters the restaurant area.*

ALISON: Hi.

DIANE: Oh hi.

ALISON: Am I late?

DIANE: No I just got here myself. Sorry but I went ahead and ordered a salad. I didn't eat any breakfast.

ALISON: That's fine.

DIANE: You look good. You look rested. When did you get back?

ALISON: A month and… Almost two months.

DIANE: Italy really stays with you though doesn't it. I spoke to Thomas last night.

ALISON: Oh yeah.

DIANE: He said to say hi.

ALISON: Hi back.

DIANE: You look good, you really do.

ALISON: So do you.

DIANE: Oh I'm an old hag. Today. You should have seen me yesterday! I was that close to twentysomething. But you know what they say.

ALISON: Close only counts in horseshoes and hand grenades.

DIANE: And elevators.

> *A beat. The* WAITER *arrives with* DIANE's *salad and water for* ALISON.

WAITER: Here you go.

DIANE: Oh great thanks.

WAITER: *(To ALISON.)* Have you decided?

ALISON: *(Re salad.)* That looks good.

DIANE: Just a salad?

ALISON: I'm not that hungry.

DIANE: Do you want some bread? I can't I'm off wheat.

ALISON: No thanks—my appetite is…I've had this headache since yesterday.

DIANE: Oh.

ALISON: It's nothing it's nothing.

DIANE: You sure?

ALISON: Yes yes. *(To the WAITER.)* Just a salad.

DIANE: And I'll have the poached salmon.

WAITER: *(Taking menus.)* All right. Thank you.

              The WAITER exits.

DIANE: Thanks for seeing me. Um.

ALISON: No that's—

DIANE: I just wanted to talk to you about um. Thomas wants us to get married. Imagine that. And I think ah well what the hell you know—and he wants to adopt Rebecca, you know legally—which I think is probably a good idea—you know for her security, and she loves Thomas. But I just wanted to mention that to you because I'm not sure how Jerry would take it. I mean he isn't really around at all, he hardly ever sees her.

ALISON: No it makes sense.

DIANE: No it does I think. And also you know I just wanted to say that I really appreciate you you know being a presence in Rebecca's life. It's been good. She likes you.

ALISON: Oh well that's… Thanks.

DIANE: As strange as it's all been.

ALISON: As strange as it's all been.

DIANE: And you know Jerry got married again.

ALISON: Yeah, last year.

DIANE: No again again.

ALISON: You're kidding.

DIANE: Practice makes perfect. Look I'm just going to make a quick call—I'm trying to change an audition time for tomorrow.

ALISON: An audition?

DIANE: Oh it's nothing really—a trip to Italy and a new frock basically.

DIANE rises. She stops.

DIANE: It looks like there's going to be a Christmas after all.

DIANE laughs. ALISON takes the flower from the vase on the table and hands it to DIANE. DIANE takes it and looks at ALISON. After a moment DIANE smiles and rips the flower in two, she gives one half to ALISON. ALISON takes the flower and then smiling throws it at DIANE. DIANE throws her half at ALISON. They are both laughing. DIANE exits. ALISON is alone a moment. The sound in the restaurant gets louder, her headache grows more severe. The WAITER returns with water. We can barely hear him over the din. ALISON's head is pounding. She rises from the table. The sound continues to build. The lights begin to strobe.

WAITER: Are you all right? Ma'am? Are you all right?

> *The strobe becomes prolonged. ALISON steps out of the reality of the restaurant and downstage toward the still-present bottle of sand. As the sound continues to build. She pulls the cork out of the bottle and slowly pours it onto the floor. When the bottle is empty a woman enters. The sound suddenly stops. The woman is CONNIE HOY. The light returns to normal.*

ALISON: Hello?

CONNIE: Hi Alison.

ALISON: Oh my God.

CONNIE: Hi, it's Connie Hoy.

ALISON: I know, oh my God.

CONNIE: Welcome. *(To Audience.)* Hi. We're just going to be another few minutes. *(To ALISON.)* Everything's okay?

ALISON: I don't know.

CONNIE: Everything's okay.

ALISON: I've been so awful to you.

CONNIE: Hm?

ALISON: I've been so awful to you.

CONNIE: Yes you've carried me with you all this time. But that had nothing to do with me, that was all about you. Anyway you'll have lots of time to deal with that later. Alison? Where are you?

ALISON: Where am I?

CONNIE: Yes.

ALISON: I don't know.

CONNIE: You can be anywhere you like. Where would you like to be? A forest? A desert? A place with a river or a lake?

ALISON: A…place with a lake.

CONNIE: Okay. Good. So be there.

ALISON: Be there?

CONNIE: Don't think about it too much. Close your eyes and just be there. Are you there?

ALISON: Okay.

CONNIE: All right. Okay. How old are you?

ALISON: I don't know…

CONNIE: You can be as old as you want to be.

ALISON: Okay. Eighty…two.

CONNIE: Fine. What time of day is it?

ALISON: Dusk. Just before dusk.

CONNIE: Summer or?

ALISON: October.

CONNIE: Are you alone?

ALISON: Yes. No. I'm with someone.

            CONNIE HOY disappears. RICHARD appears.

ALISON: Someone I love.

RICHARD: It's chilly.

            ALISON turns to look at RICHARD. He places a shawl on her shoulders.

            It's chilly.

ALISON: Yes.

RICHARD: The leaves are turning late again.

ALISON: Yes.

RICHARD: I've been thinking.

ALISON: Yes?

RICHARD: You know what I'm going to do one of these days?

ALISON: What?

RICHARD: I'm going to get myself some long-sleeved T-shirts.

ALISON: What do you mean?

RICHARD: Some of those long-sleeved T-shirts, I'm going to get some for myself.

ALISON: But you don't like anything on your arms.

RICHARD: I know.

ALISON: You won't even wear a watch.

RICHARD: I know. But my arms get cold you know.

ALISON: Are you cold?

RICHARD: I do. My arms do get cold.

ALISON: Maybe that's not a bad idea then. Some long-sleeved T-shirts.

RICHARD: That's what I was thinking.

ALISON: Are you cold now?

RICHARD: No it's pleasant.

ALISON: Yes.

RICHARD: It's nice isn't it.

ALISON: Yes. It is.

RICHARD: You don't want to go inside do you?

ALISON: No I'm fine here.

> *ALISON looks out at the lake and smiles.*

It's nice.

> *Fade to black.*

> *The End.*